This Guide Wi

l:

1. Get started

2. Eat right

3. Be active

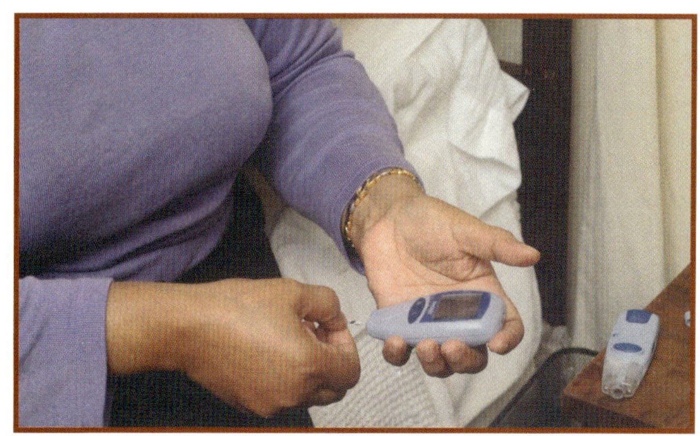

4. Check your blood sugar

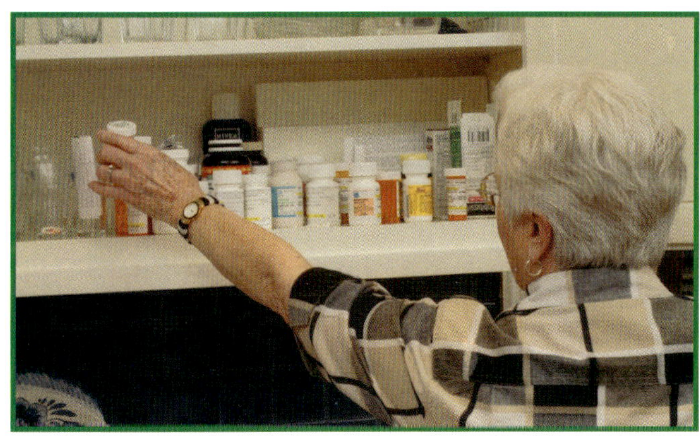

5. Take your pills

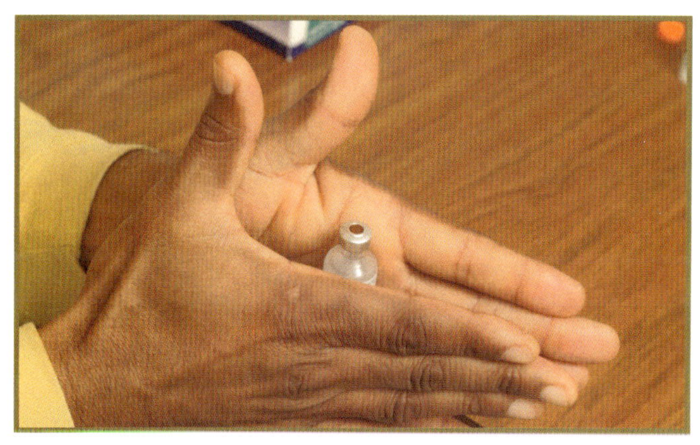

6. Learn about insulin

Chapter 1: Get Started

When you have diabetes, taking care of yourself is important. Your doctor and health care team are here to help you. However, most of your day-to-day diabetes care is up to you and your family.

Having diabetes is life-changing.

People with diabetes say they sometimes feel overwhelmed. Some people feel alone.

You are not alone.

Millions of people have diabetes.

This guide will give you the information you need to live a better life with diabetes.

What's in it for you?

By learning to take care of yourself, you will have more energy and feel better.

This book will help you get started. You might surprise yourself at just how good you'll feel!

Facts About Diabetes

• When you have diabetes, your body has a harder time changing the food you eat into the energy you need.

• Diabetes causes sugar to build up in the blood. If the sugar stays high, it can slowly damage the heart, kidneys, eyes, and feet.

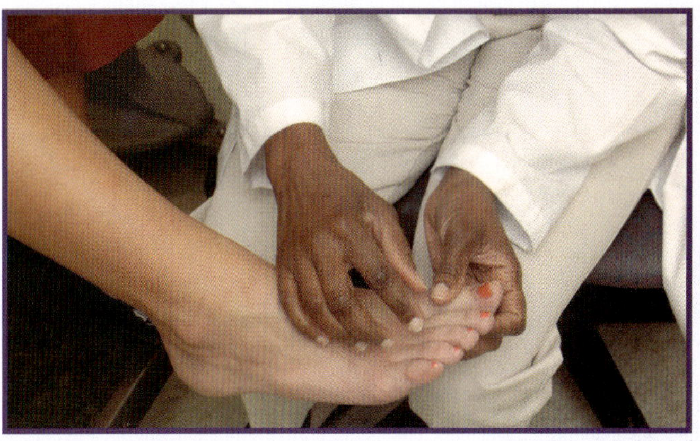

• Diabetes is a life-long disease, but you can control it by eating right and moving your body more. Most people also have to take pills or insulin shots.

• It takes time and practice to learn how to do these things. You and your health care team can work together to find the best way to control your diabetes.

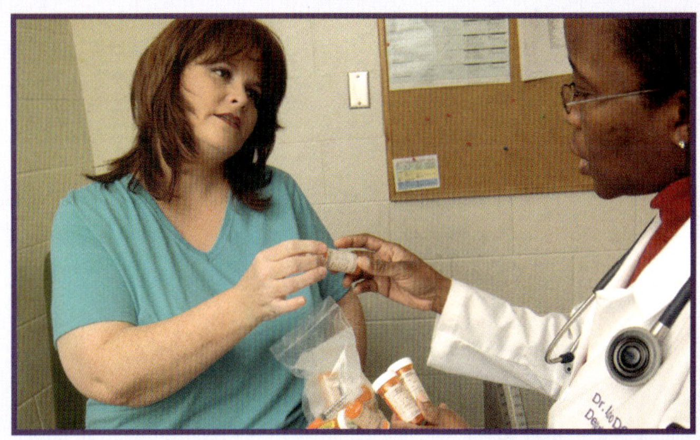

• People with diabetes often have other health problems. Stopping smoking, controlling your blood pressure, and getting help with depression will help your diabetes.

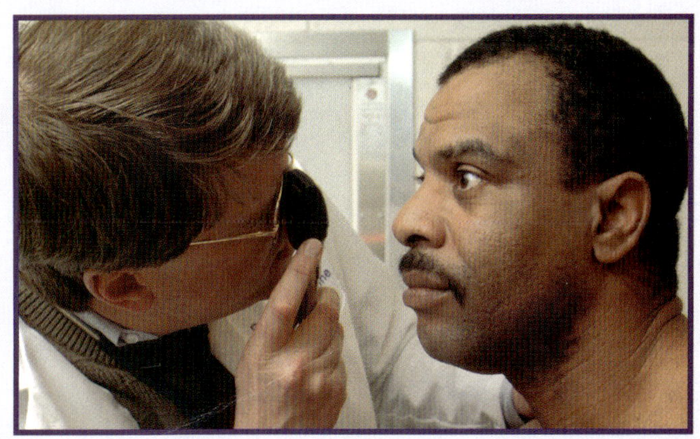

• Use this guide to learn the skills you need to take charge of your diabetes and live the life you want to live. You can take this one step at a time. **Just START.** Share this guide with family and friends and get their support.

Chapter 2: Eat Right

Eating right is the most important way to control your blood sugar. Your blood sugar is affected by what you eat, when you eat, and how much you eat.

The good news is that you don't have to go hungry, buy special foods, or give up all your favorite foods.

Two things you must do:

1. Eat smaller portions.
2. Eat fewer carbohydrates like sweets and starches.

What's in it for you?

• Eating the right portion sizes may help you lose weight.

• Most people with diabetes will feel better if they lose even a few pounds. Losing weight will also help lower your blood sugar.

Watch Your Portion Sizes

• Many people do not realize that the portion sizes they now eat are too big. One of the most important ways to control your blood sugar is to eat the right portion sizes.

Look at these plates. The plates on the left have too much food. The portions are too big. The ones on the right have the correct amount of food.

TOO MUCH

RIGHT SIZE

TOO MUCH

RIGHT SIZE

Helpful Tips About Portion Sizes

"A correct portion of meat is about the same size as a deck of cards."

"When I eat out, I box up half my meal. Now it's like I get two meals for the price of one. I save money, and I do not overeat!"

"I love fruit, but I don't overdo it. I eat an apple or a pear about the size of a tennis ball."

"I am a meat and potatoes man. I eat a potato about the size of my fist. I like to spice it up with pepper and even salsa."

"I fill a teacup with cooked rice to get the right portion size. The teacup is always handy for me."

"I like the taste of salad dressing, butter and gravy. But I go easy on them now and use half as much."

Still Hungry?

- One way to feel full with smaller portions is to eat slowly.
- Take at least 20 minutes to eat each meal.
- Taste each bite of your food. Your meal will be more enjoyable.
- Wait a few minutes before getting a second helping. You may find you're no longer hungry.

Drink more water.
- Drink a glass before you eat.
- Take a sip between each bite.

Eat more vegetables.

Take a short walk after meals.

The Healthy Plate

Think of your plate as 3 different sections:
one section for vegetables, one for protein, and one for carbohydrates (carbs).

Carbohydrates (Carbs)

• Carbohydrates (which include fruits, sweets, and starches) make your blood sugar go up more than most other foods. Pasta, potatoes, rice, beans, tortillas, desserts and even milk are high in carbs.

• The good news is that you don't have to cut carbs out. Eating the right portion size is what's important. Here are examples of carbs that are too much and the right sizes.

TOO MUCH RIGHT SIZE

TOO MUCH RIGHT SIZE

Remember:

You can still eat carbs, just make the portion sizes smaller.

Desserts Have Carbs

Desserts have a lot of carbs. All carbs make your blood sugar go up. Ask your doctor if you can have a little bit of dessert.

What is a small portion of dessert?

- 1 small scoop of ice cream
- 1 snack size (mini) candy bar
- 1 small piece of cake

"When my sugar levels are OK, I can eat a small piece of cake."

"Even when candy says sugar-free, I keep my portions small. I learned that sugar-free does not mean I can eat all I want."

"I like to eat something sweet after dinner. So now I eat a small piece of fruit instead of cookies or cake."

Drinks Have Carbs

Many drinks are high in carbs. Juices, fruit drinks, sodas, and even milk make your blood sugar go up.

What are the best drinks for you?

- diet sodas or sugar-free drinks
- tea or coffee
  (with sugar substitutes if you want)
- water
- low fat or skim milk
  (no more than two glasses a day)

Alcoholic drinks can make it hard for you to control your blood sugar. If you drink alcohol, don't have more than 2 drinks a day. Talk to your doctor about how to drink alcohol safely.

Proteins

Proteins include meat, fish, chicken and tofu. Eating well also means eating the right portions of proteins. Below are examples of meals with proteins in the right portion sizes.

Proteins are good for your body. They keep blood sugar even and keep you from getting hungry between meals.

Vegetables

The good news is most vegetables are low in carbs, so you can eat as much of these as you want.

Broccoli

Cabbage

Spinach

Green Salad

Carrots

Celery

Zucchini

Peppers

Cucumbers

Jicama

Mushrooms

Tomatoes

Watch out! These vegetables are starchy and are high in carbs! Keep the portion sizes small.

Potatoes

Corn

Sweet Potatoes

French Fries

Putting It All Together

Wake up to a good breakfast!

• Eating breakfast will help fill you up and give you energy. It will also help you control your diabetes.

• You need to eat carbohydrate and protein at breakfast. For protein, try eggs or egg substitute, sugar-free yogurt, or cottage cheese.

• Only have bacon or sausage once in a while. When you do, try turkey bacon or sausage.

• If you are in a hurry, eat a piece of toast with some peanut butter on it.

• Eating protein will give you more energy and help keep you from getting hungry later in the day.

"I am a busy person and used to skip breakfast. Now I eat a little something in the morning, and I have more energy."

Let's do lunch!

It is best to make your lunch at home because you can control your portion size. When you eat out, order a small size instead of a "super size".

"I like to eat soup for lunch. It fills me up without a lot of carbs!"

"I stopped buying those combo meals. I get the regular size now and order a diet drink or water."

"I always ask for a to-go box. I save half my sandwich for my next meal."

Dinner is served!

No matter where you eat dinner, remember your divided plate. Imagine your plate in 3 sections: vegetables, proteins and carbs.

"If I go to a buffet, I remember the divided plate and only fill it once. If I want more, I go for fresh salad with a little bit of dressing."

"When I go for seconds, I go for the vegetables. They really fill me up."

Snack attack!

What should you do when you get hungry between meals? Snack on these:

Veggie Sticks

Sugar-free Gum

Hardboiled Eggs

Unbuttered Popcorn

Keep foods like these close by so you can get to them easily when you feel hungry. Stay away from foods that are high in carbs or sugar (like chips, crackers, candy bars, or pretzels).

"I keep a little bag of nuts in my desk at work. I snack on them in the afternoon."

"I eat sugar-free gelatin for my snack and dessert. It is so easy to make!"

You *Can* Do It

Choose one of these easy ideas or write down 1 or 2 things you will do for the next few weeks. Remember, little changes in your eating can make a big difference in your blood sugar.

- ❑ I will switch from juice or soda to diet soda.
- ❑ I will eat breakfast every morning.
- ❑ I will order regular size instead of super size at fast-food restaurants.
- ❑ I will pack a healthy lunch some days instead of eating out.
- ❑ I will keep healthy snacks on hand, like cottage cheese, carrot sticks, hard-boiled eggs, unbuttered popcorn, or sugar-free popsicles.
- ❑ I will eat slowly and wait before getting a second serving.
- ❑ ______________________________
- ❑ ______________________________
- ❑ ______________________________

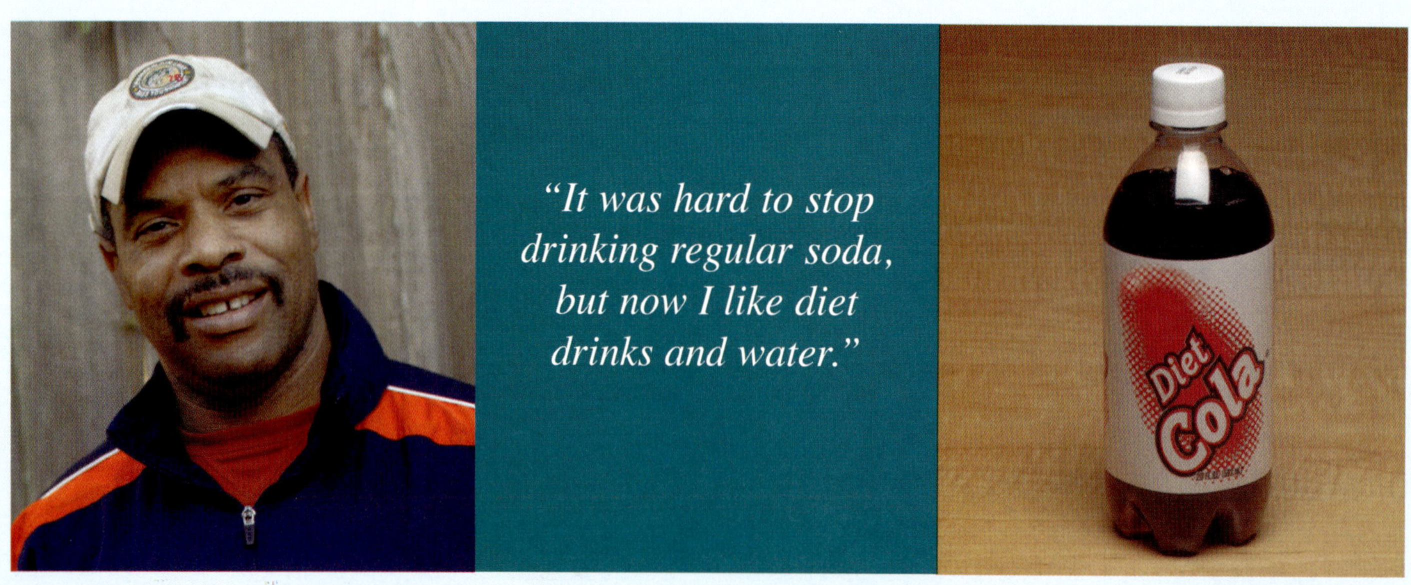

"It was hard to stop drinking regular soda, but now I like diet drinks and water."

Chapter 3: Be Active

What's in it for you?

- Being more active is one of the best things you can do to control your blood sugar.
- Moving more can help you lose weight, have more energy, and feel more upbeat.
- No matter how old you are, being active is good for you.

Start smart!

If you are not exercising, start with 10 minutes a day. It can be as simple as walking 5 minutes from your door and turning around and walking back.

You might be surprised that some of the activities you can do everyday are exercise:

- Climbing stairs
- Housework like sweeping, vacuuming, dusting
- Mowing the lawn or working in your garden
- Walking to the bus

Some people exercise by:

- Using a stationary bicycle
- Walking in the mall
- Enrolling in water aerobics
- Going to an exercise class

A lot of people say that walking is the easiest exercise for them. Many people walk with a friend or their pet. Walking is free, easy, and fun.

So turn off the TV, get up and get moving!

Helpful Tips If You Have Trouble Walking

- You can stretch, lift weights or do yoga while sitting in a chair. Look for videos or books at your library to help you get started.

- Stretch bands and wrist or ankle cuffs with weights can help build muscle strength. You can buy them at sports or discount stores.

- Community pools often have special water exercise classes. Call your local parks and recreation department.

"I can still sit in my chair and lift weights. I just use soup cans."

"I do what I can. I wheel myself around instead of having someone always pushing me in my wheelchair."

Helpful Tips For Getting Started

Here are some easy ways to get active every day.

"I put on my favorite music and dance for about 20 minutes. It's fun!"

"Instead of riding the elevator, I take the stairs."

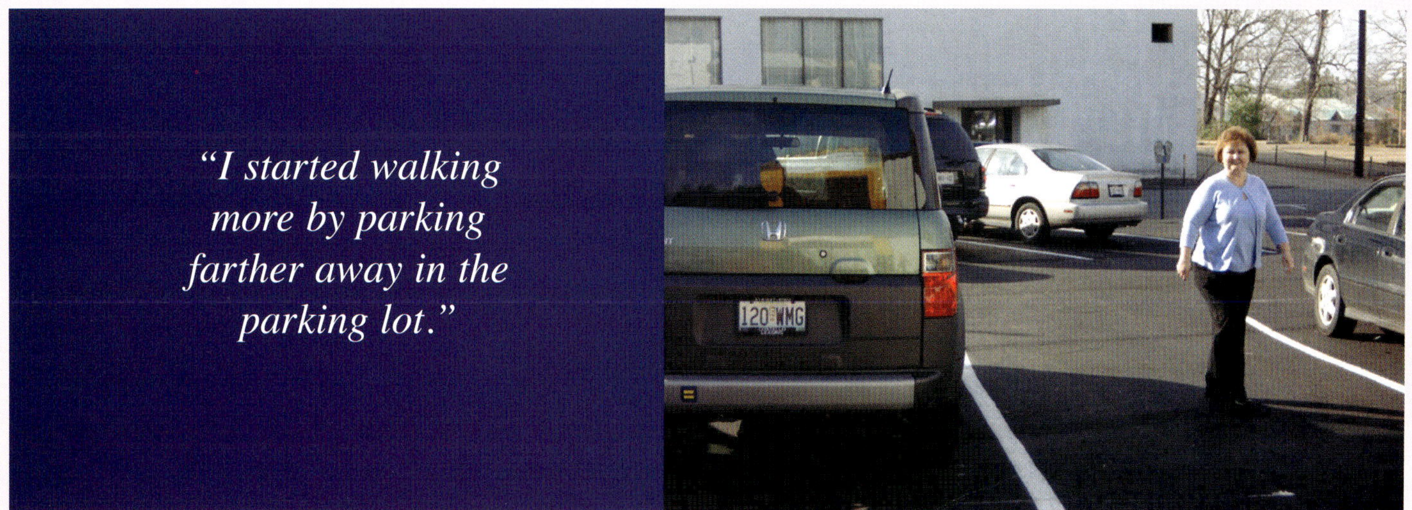

"I started walking more by parking farther away in the parking lot."

Exercise Will Get Easier

Your body needs time to get used to being more active. Be patient. It takes a few months for a new activity to become a habit.

"I wear a pedometer that counts the steps I take. I started at 1000 steps a day. Every week I try to add another 500 steps, and now I'm up to 4000."

Steps for doing more:

- Begin by doing an activity for 10 minutes, two times per week.

- After a couple of weeks, add 2-5 minutes a day.

- When you feel comfortable doing more, add another day.

- You want to work up to 30 minutes of exercise at least 3-4 times a week.

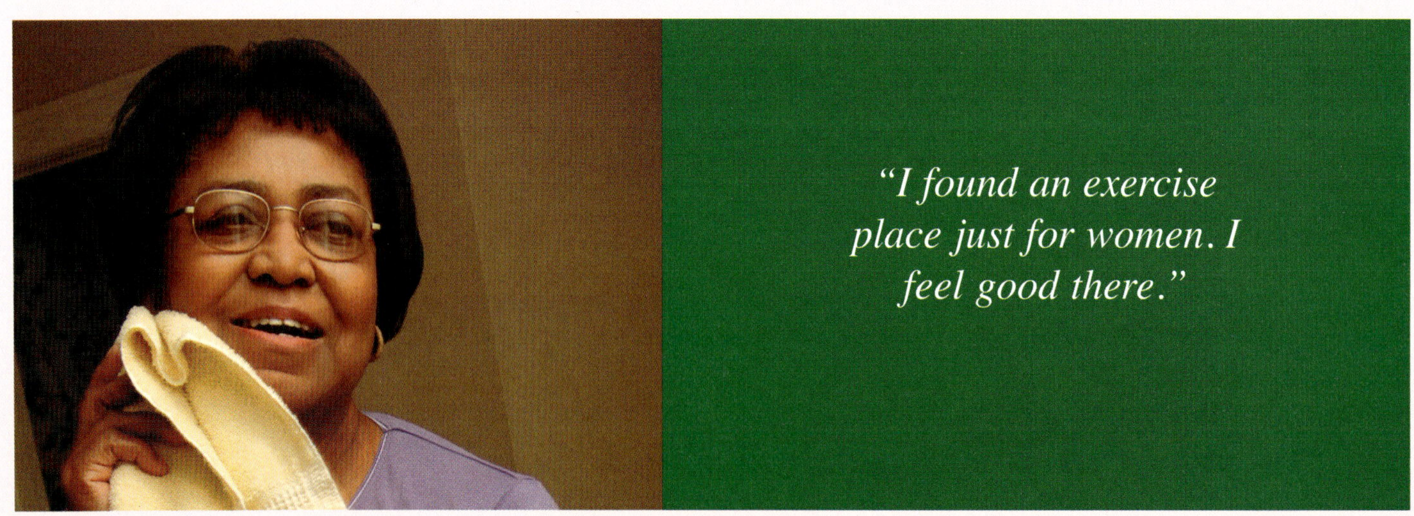

"I found an exercise place just for women. I feel good there."

Be Safe

• Exercise with a friend or partner, if possible.

• Start slowly. Stop if you feel any pain or have trouble catching your breath.

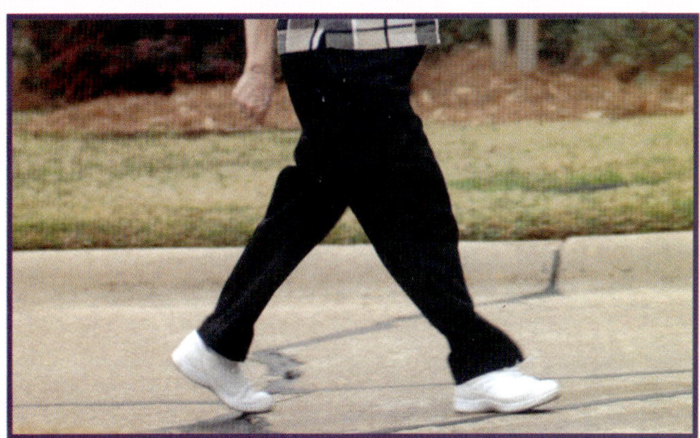

• Wear shoes that fit well, and always check your feet for sores when you are finished exercising

• Carry some "emergency sugar" in your pocket in case your blood sugar drops too low. A few packets of sugar or honey, a mini box of raisins, or some glucose tablets work well.

• Drink a lot of water. If you can't have water with you when you exercise, drink a glass before you begin and a glass when you are finished.

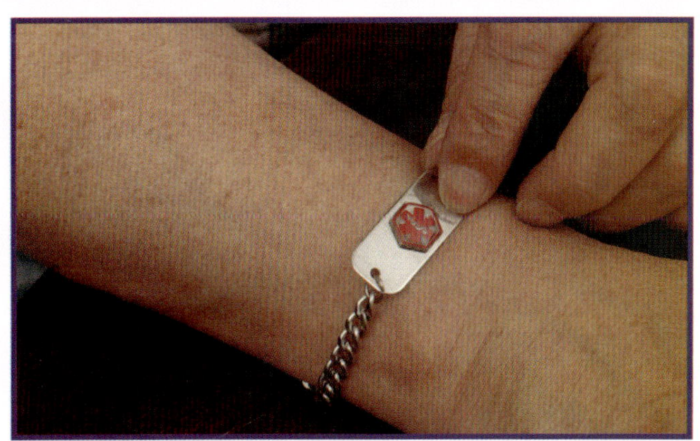

• Carry something with you that says you have diabetes. Your doctor can help you get a bracelet or a card for your wallet.

You *Can* Do It

Pick things YOU like to do. Try one of these suggestions, or write down 1 or 2 things you enjoy that make your body move.

- ❑ I will take a short walk every day.
- ❑ I will park farther away in a parking lot.
- ❑ I will dance for 20 minutes at home.
- ❑ I will get up and do small chores during TV commercials.
- ❑ I will take the stairs instead of the elevator.
- ❑ I will stretch for ten minutes when I wake up each day.
- ❑ ______________________________
- ❑ ______________________________

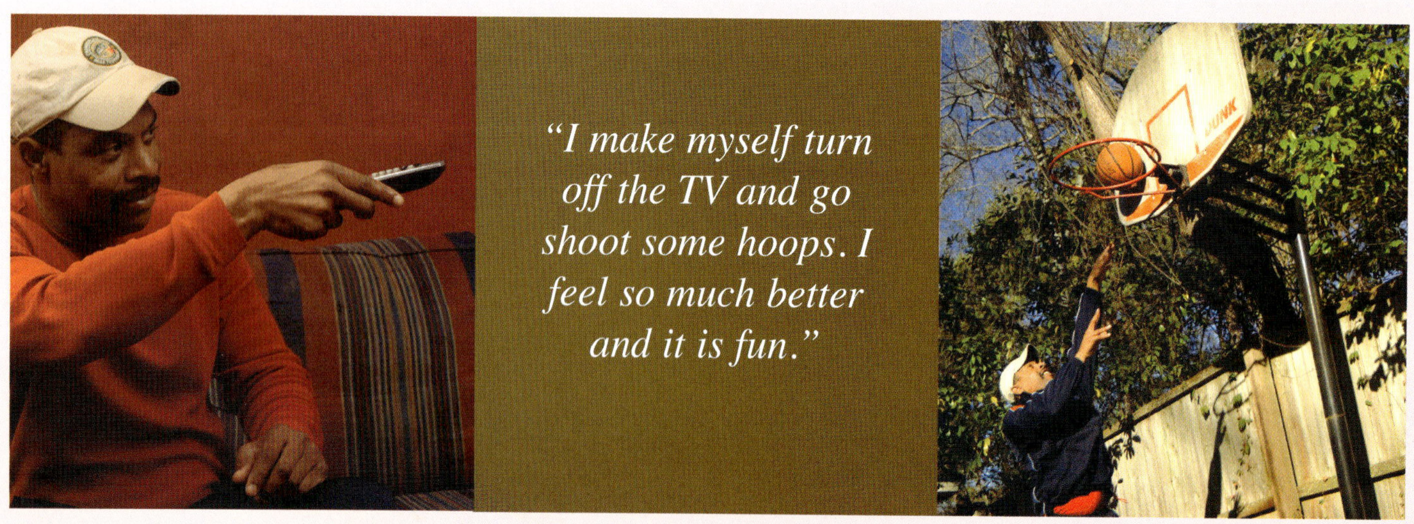

Chapter 4: Check Your Blood Sugar

Your body turns the food you eat into blood sugar. Blood sugar (or blood glucose) is what gives your body energy.

If your blood sugar is too low, your body does not have the energy it needs. It is very important to get your blood sugar back to normal quickly.

If your blood sugar is high for too long, it can damage your eyes, kidneys, heart and feet.

What's in it for you?

- If you know your blood sugar is too low or too high, then you can take action to fix it. This will help keep your blood sugar normal.
- If your blood sugar is normal, you will feel better.

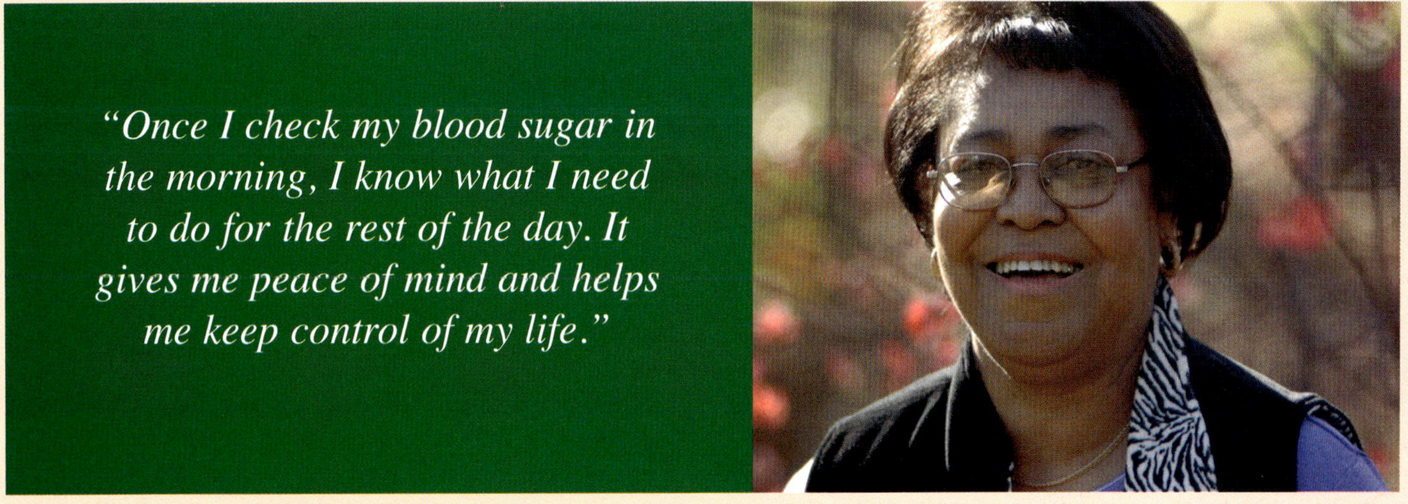

What do you need to know about your blood sugar machine?

Your blood sugar machine *(also called a meter or monitor)* gives you a number that tells you what your blood sugar is.

There are many types of machines and all of them work differently.

Talk with your doctor, diabetes nurse or pharmacist to learn exactly how to use your machine.

When should you check your blood sugar?

Most people need to check their blood sugar before they eat breakfast. You may also need to check it at other times.

You and your doctor can decide what is best for you.

Check your blood sugar if you:
- feel it is too high or too low
- feel sick

"I used to think I could tell what my blood sugar was without checking it. But really, the only way I can tell is by using my monitor."

Helpful Tips About Checking Your Blood Sugar

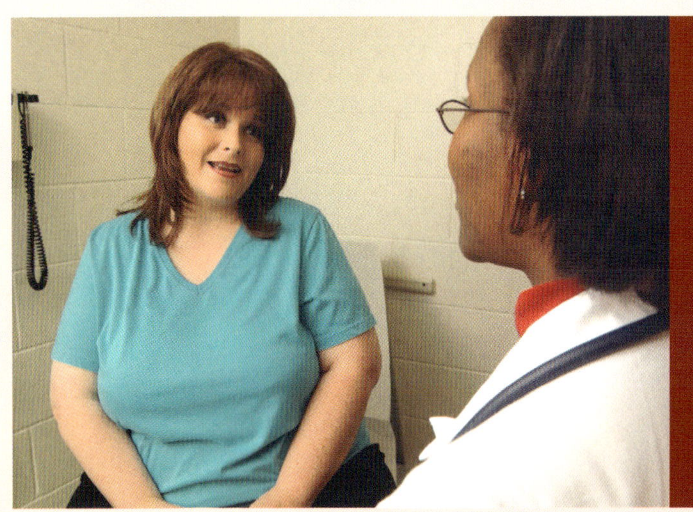

"At first I tried to use my blood sugar machine, but I couldn't get it to work. Then my doctor showed me how to use it. She told me that everyone has trouble at first."

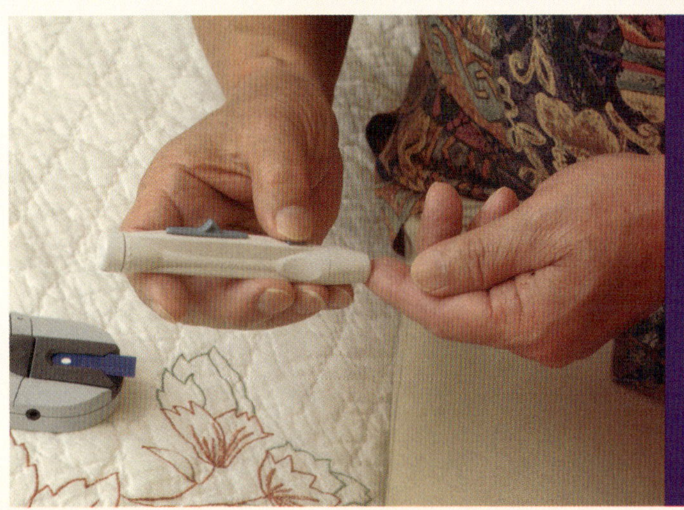

"Pricking my finger hurt. The nurse showed me how to prick it on the side instead of in the middle. That made a big difference."

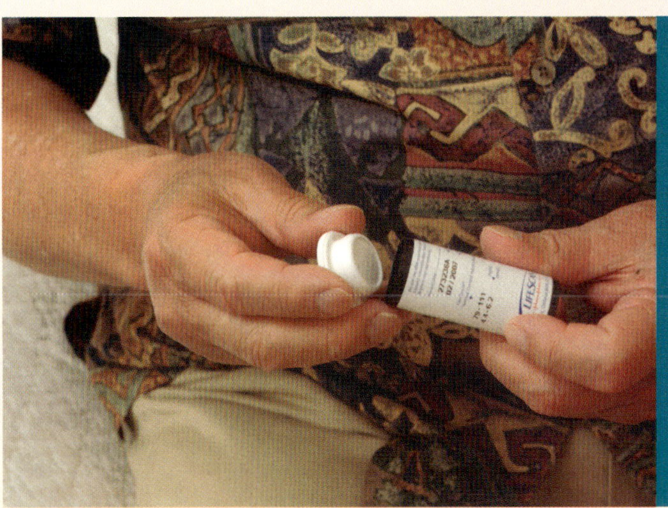

"I didn't want to tell my doctor that I couldn't afford the test strips. But when I did, she found a way to help me."

Blood Sugar Lows

How low is "too low"?

Blood sugar less than 70 is too low for everybody. For some people, blood sugar less than 80 or 90 may be too low. Talk with your doctor to decide what is too low for you.

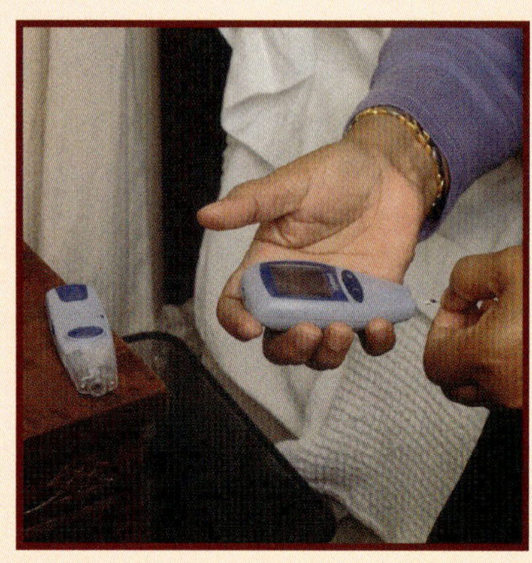

If your blood sugar is too low, you may feel:

- Shaky or nervous
- Sweaty or clammy
- Dizzy or confused
- Tired or hungry

Watch out!

People have different feelings when their blood sugar is too low. If you are not feeling right, you should check your blood sugar.

If your blood sugar is too low, ask yourself:

- Did I skip a meal or eat my meal later than usual?
- Did I eat less than usual or fewer carbs than usual?
- Did I exercise more than usual?
- Did I take too much medicine?
- Did my doctor just change my medicines?

All of these things can make your blood sugar go down.

Talk to your doctor about your low blood sugars at every visit.

What should you do if you feel like your blood sugar is too low?

Check your blood sugar right away. If your blood sugar is below 70, you need to do these things ***immediately***:

1. Get sugar into your body quickly. Drink half a glass of juice or regular soda, or eat some candy with sugar (chew it, don't suck it!).

2. Then, eat a small snack with protein, such as half of a sandwich or cheese and crackers.

3. Check your blood sugar again in 15 minutes to see if it has gone up.

4. If it is still too low, drink more juice or eat another piece of candy. Then call your doctor.

If your blood sugar is too low, it is very important to ***do something about it***, even if you do not feel bad. If it continues to fall, you could pass out.

Call 911 or go to the emergency room if you feel too sick to get a snack, or if after 30 minutes your blood sugar is not above 80.

Blood Sugar Highs

How high is "too high"?

For most people, blood sugar more than 140 or 150 is too high. Blood sugar more than 200 is too high for everybody. Talk with your doctor to decide what your blood sugar should be.

If your blood sugar gets too high you may:

- Feel very thirsty
- Start peeing more than usual
- Feel weak or tired
- Get blurry vision
- Feel just like you usually do

Ask yourself these questions:

- Did I eat more carbs than usual?
- Did I skip any of my medicines?
- Did I get less exercise than usual?
- Have I been under a lot of stress lately?

All of these things can make your blood sugar go up.

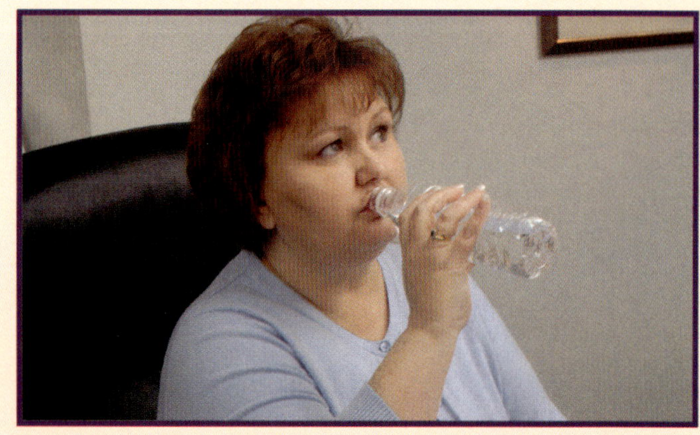

What should you do if your blood sugar is too high?

- Drink lots of water, even if it feels like you are peeing too much.
- Cut down on carbs until your blood sugar comes down.

Putting It All Together

1. Always write down your blood sugar numbers in a log.

Show it to your doctor every time you visit.

2. Know your numbers.

For most people blood sugar should be:

80-120	first thing in morning and before meals
100-140	at bedtime

Ask your doctor to tell you what your blood sugar should be:

______ before meals

______ at bedtime

3. Talk to your doctor.

If your blood sugar is too high or too low more than once a week, call your doctor.

Ask your doctor to tell you what blood sugar is too high or too low for you:

______ too high

______ too low

You *Can* Do It

Remember that you are the most important person to manage your diabetes! Choose one of these ideas or write down 1 or 2 ways to help you take control of your blood sugar.

- ❑ I will check my blood sugar every morning, or as my doctor tells me to.
- ❑ I will write down my blood sugar numbers in my blood sugar log and take it to all my doctor visits.
- ❑ I will keep candy with me in case of an emergency.
- ❑ ______________________________
- ❑ ______________________________

One other thing to think about

The A1c test

This is a blood test you get at the doctor's office. It gives your doctor an idea of what your blood sugars have been over the last three months. Ask your doctor what you A1c should be: __________

"Keeping my blood sugar in control can be tricky. But when I know what it is, I can do something to fix it!"

Chapter 5: Take Your Pills

• Most people with diabetes need to take one or more pills to keep their blood sugar normal.

• You may also need medicines for other health problems like high cholesterol or high blood pressure. It can be hard to keep track of so many pills. This guide will help you.

• Remember, it is OK to ask your family or friends for help.

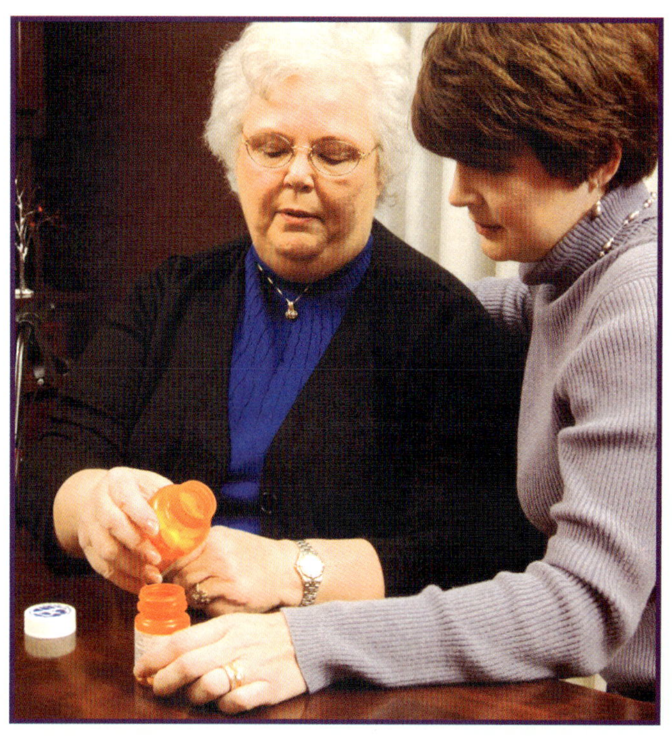

Safety First

Taking your pills safely will help you feel better.

• Take your pills at the same time every day. This helps keep your blood sugar from getting too high or too low.

• Don't skip meals or your pills may make your blood sugar go too low.

• Don't stop taking your medicines unless your doctor tells you to. Call your doctor if your medicines:

- don't have refills
- make you feel sick
- are too expensive
- make your blood sugar too low

• Take your medicine bottles to every doctor's visit. That way you and your doctor can keep better track of your medicines.

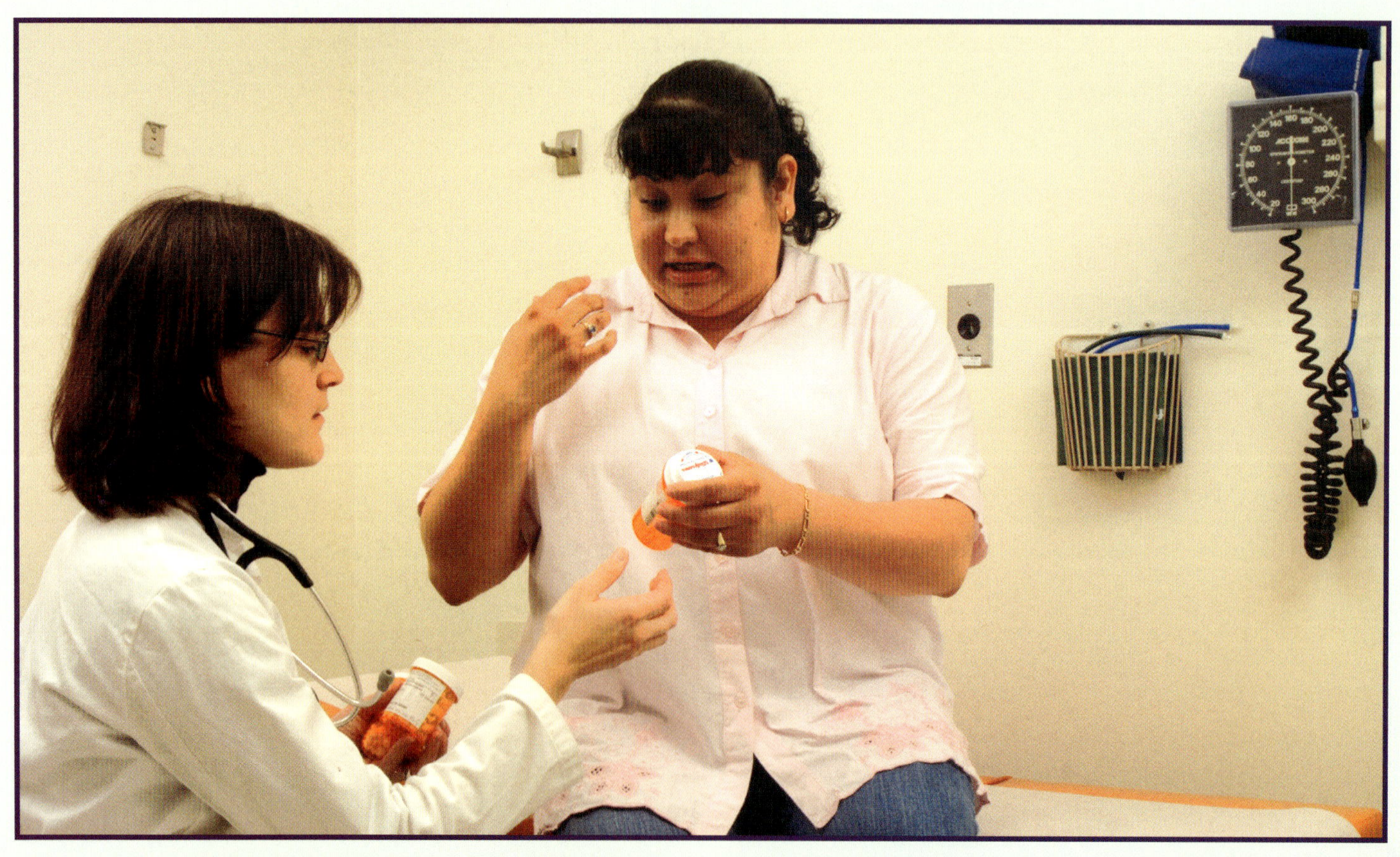

Helpful Tips For Keeping Track Of Your Pills

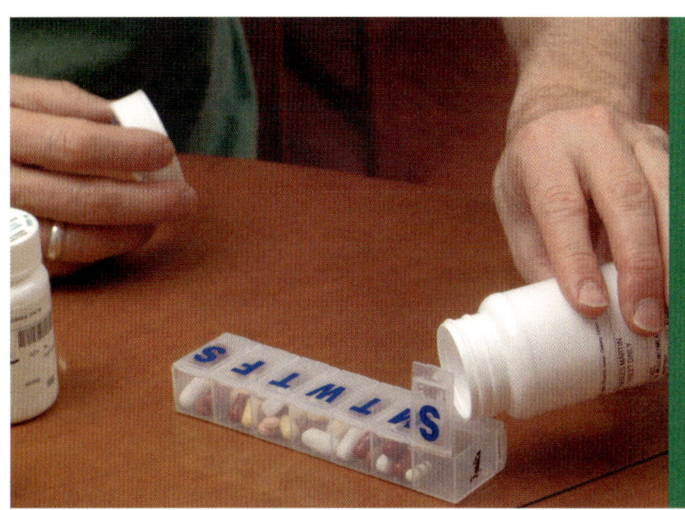

"I have a pill box to remind me if I have taken my pills each day."

"My son and I made a calendar of all the medicines I take. This makes it easy."

"I bring a list of the pills I am taking to my doctor. This helps her understand me better."

You *Can* Do It

Remember, taking your pills safely can make a big difference in your blood sugar. Choose one of these easy ideas or write down 1 or 2 ways of keeping track of your pills.

- ❑ I will take my medicine bottles to my next doctor's appointment.
- ❑ I will use a pill box to help me keep track of my pills.
- ❑ I will ask my family to help me keep up with my pills.
- ❑ I will ask my pharmacist for a list of all my medicines and what they are for.
- ❑ I will make a list of my pills and keep it in my wallet.
- ❑ ______________________________
- ❑ ______________________________

"I stopped taking my medicine because it gave me diarrhea, but I didn't want to tell my doctor. When I told him, he wasn't upset. He just changed my medicine!"

"I was worried I couldn't pay for my medicines. When I told my doctor, she helped me find a way."

Chapter 6: Learn About Insulin

Before you had diabetes, your body made enough insulin to keep your blood sugar normal. Now that you have diabetes, you may need to take extra insulin to help control your blood sugar.

There are many different types of insulin. Most are given with a shot.

• Some types of insulin last all day, and others last for only a few hours.

• Your doctor or nurse will explain to you what type of insulin you take and how to take it.

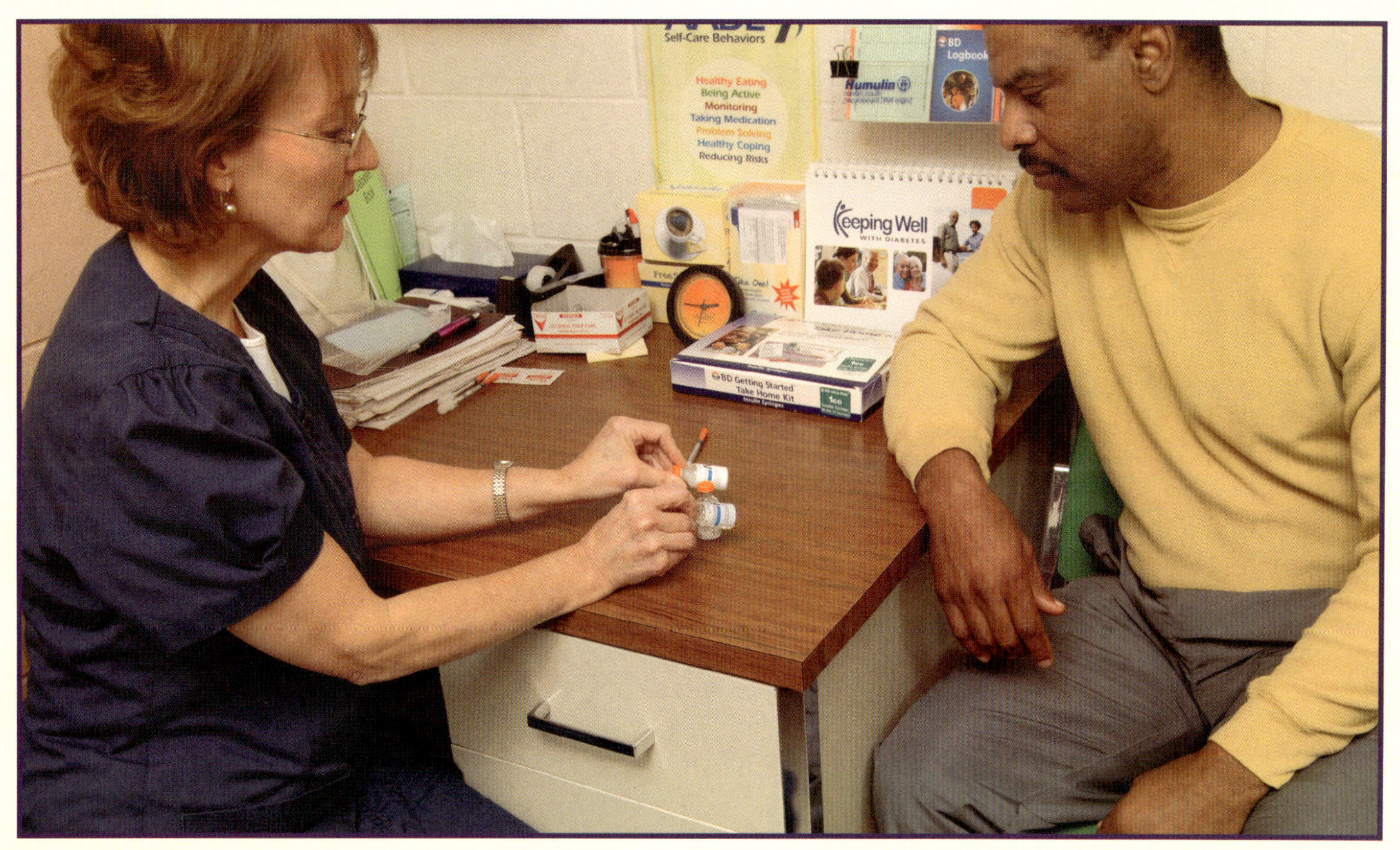

Feeling like you failed?

Many people feel like they have failed if they can't control their blood sugar with pills. This is not true. For many people, insulin shots are the only way to keep blood sugar levels normal. You are not a failure if you have to use insulin.

Feeling worried about bad things happening?

Insulin will NOT cause bad things to happen to your kidneys, eyes or feet. Taking insulin safely helps prevent these problems.

Feeling scared about shots?

Many people are afraid of giving themselves shots. They think it will hurt. But most people who take insulin say giving themselves shots is very easy and usually does not hurt.

"When I started taking insulin, I thought I had done something wrong after trying so hard. When my doctor told me that many people have to use insulin at some point, I felt better."

"At first I was scared of the shot, but now it's something I do every day. The needle is tiny...not like getting a shot in the doctor's office."

How To Take Insulin

1. Choose a place on your body that has some fat. These are examples of good places:
   - your stomach (not too near the belly button)
   - the back of your upper arm
   - the outsides of your thighs or hips

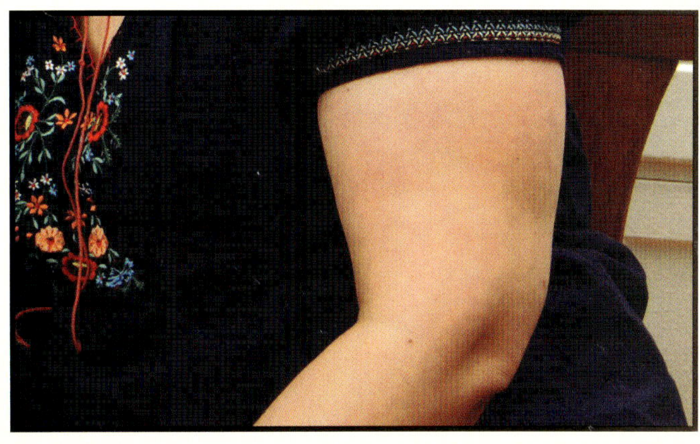

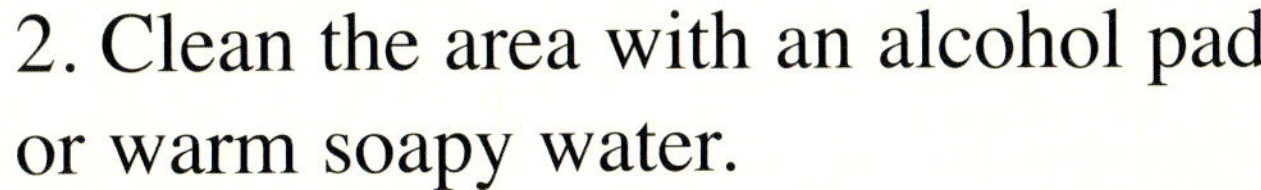

2. Clean the area with an alcohol pad or warm soapy water.

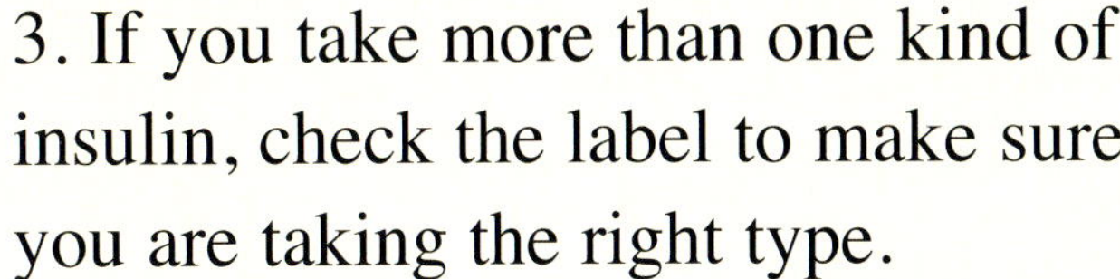

3. If you take more than one kind of insulin, check the label to make sure you are taking the right type.

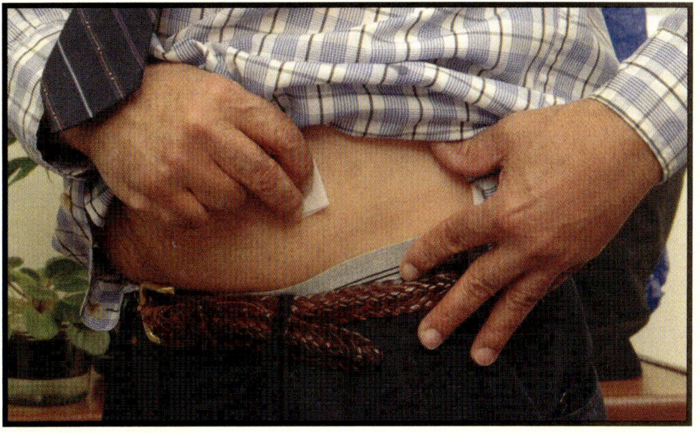

4. The first time you use the bottle, take off the plastic cap.

5. Then wipe the rubber top with an alcohol pad.

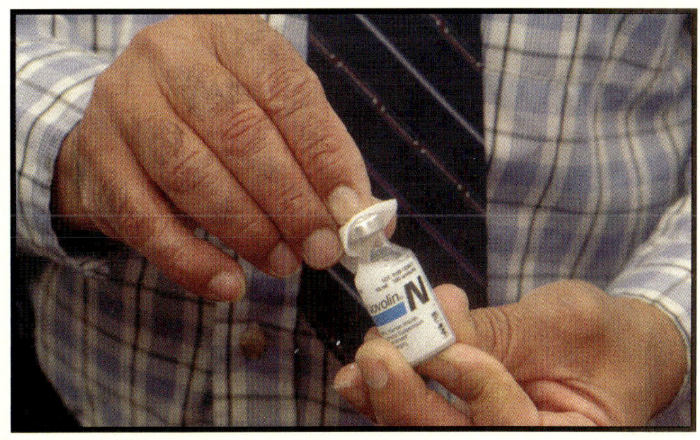

6. Note: If you take **N insulin**, it needs to be gently mixed before you take a shot. Roll it between your fingers until it looks milky.

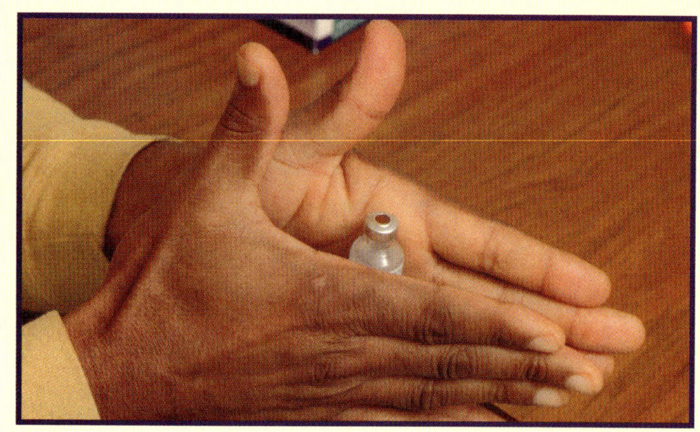

7. Uncap the needle. Draw into the syringe the same amount of air as the amount of insulin you should take.

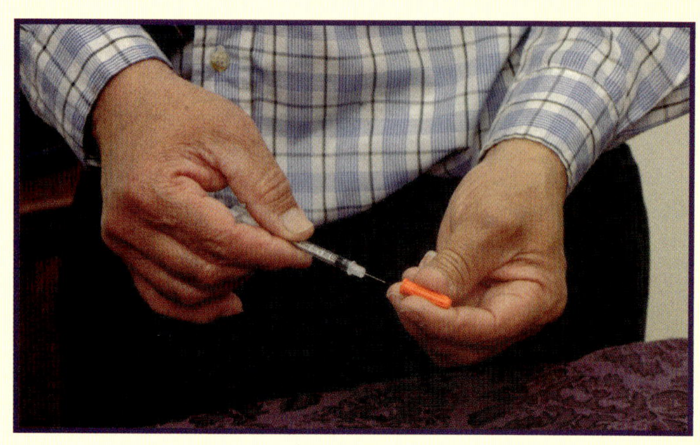

8. Push the needle through the rubber top of the insulin bottle and inject the air into the bottle. This will make it easier to pull the insulin out.

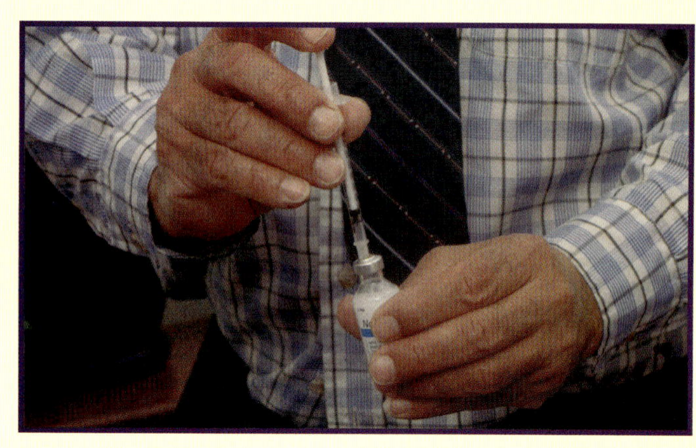

9. While the needle is still inside the bottle, turn the bottle over. Look at the numbers on the side of the syringe. Start pulling the insulin in. Stop pulling when the liquid reaches the number your doctor told you to inject.

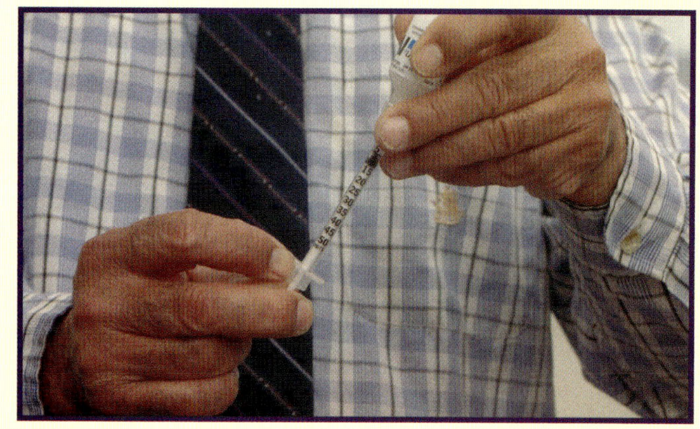

10. If you get an air bubble in your syringe, push the insulin back into the bottle. Draw it up again until you get the right dose. If you have to, tilt the bottle so the tip of the needle is in the insulin, not in air.

Watch out!

Don't push insulin back in the bottle if you take two kinds of insulin in one shot!

11. Pinch a bit of skin and stick the needle in all the way. If you don't have a lot of fat, put the needle in at an angle.

12. Push the plunger in all the way.

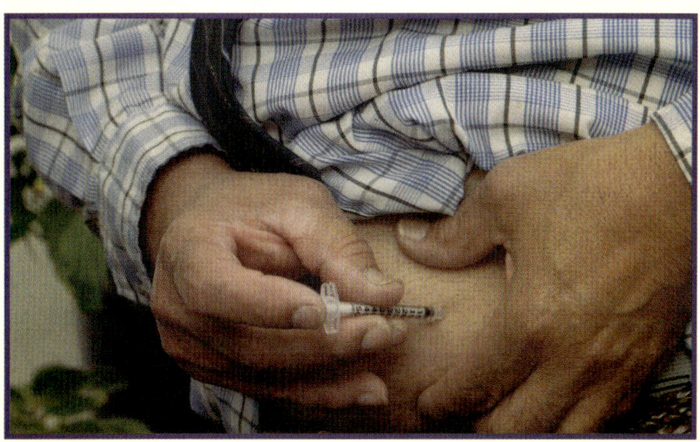

13. Pull the needle straight out. Apply light pressure with some cotton or tissue, if necessary. But do not rub the area.

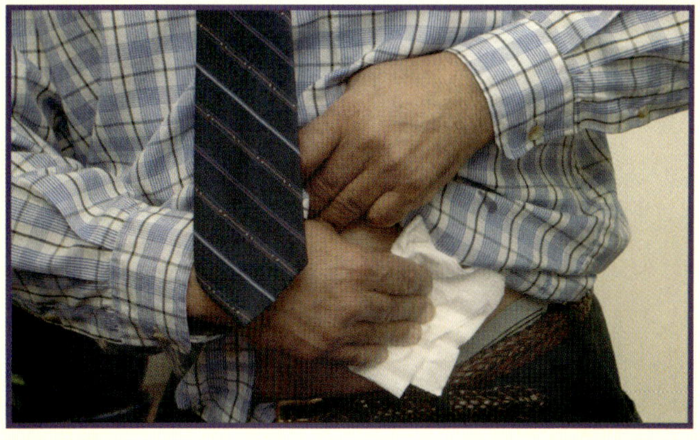

14. When you are finished, place the used needles in a plastic container, not in the trash. Your pharmacist can give you a container.

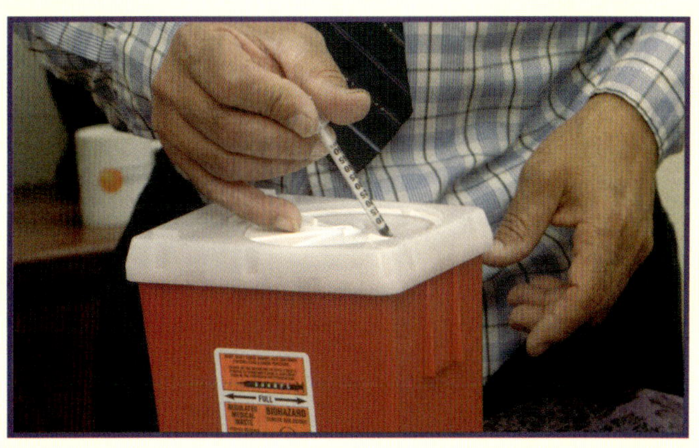

Other Things To Think About

Storing your insulin

• Keep your insulin in the refrigerator, not in the freezer or on the counter. Some types of insulin can be stored outside the refrigerator after they are opened. Talk to your doctor or pharmacist to see if you can leave yours out.

• Never leave your insulin someplace where it could get too hot, like in a parked car. Ask your doctor or nurse how to keep insulin cool if you carry it with you.

• Talk to your doctor or pharmacist about how long you can keep an open bottle. It may help to write on the bottle the date you opened it.

Traveling with insulin

• If you travel outside the USA, take your insulin and needles (syringes) with you.

• If you have to buy insulin or syringes outside the country, get help from a pharmacist or another health professional so you get the right dose.

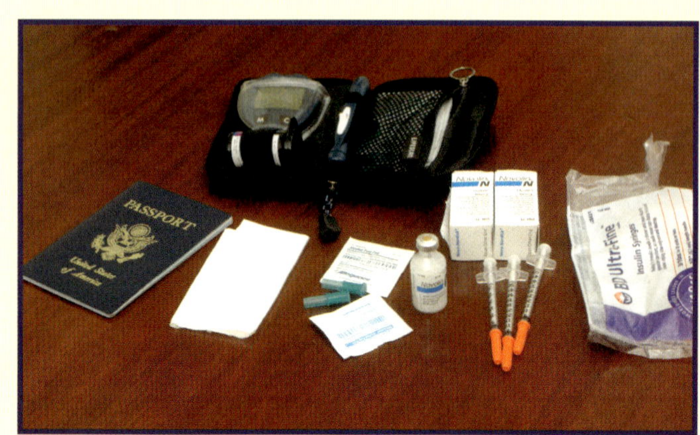

Using needles safely

• Never share your needles with anyone.
• Keep new and used needles in a safe place away from children.

You *Can* Do It

Remember, taking your insulin correctly makes a big difference in your blood sugar. Use these easy ideas, or write down your own ideas to help you feel more comfortable about taking insulin.

- ☐ I will talk with other people who take insulin shots.
- ☐ I will ask a friend or family member to stay with me the first few times I give myself a shot.
- ☐ I will practice giving shots to an orange.
- ☐ I will check my blood sugar before giving myself my insulin shot everyday.
- ☐ ______________________________

"At first, I really didn't want to take shots, but I didn't realize how much better I could feel. It made a big difference to me."

Live Well With Diabetes

Remember, you are not alone. Millions of people are living well with diabetes. Like all of the people in this book, you can take charge of your life and live successfully with diabetes.

"When I found out I had diabetes, I had to change a lot of things about the way I lived my life. Now, I am exercising and have more energy. I really feel better about myself!"

"I have taken charge of my life, and I am proud of what I have accomplished."

"Having diabetes has opened my eyes to new things. Now, I am doing things I have never done before!"

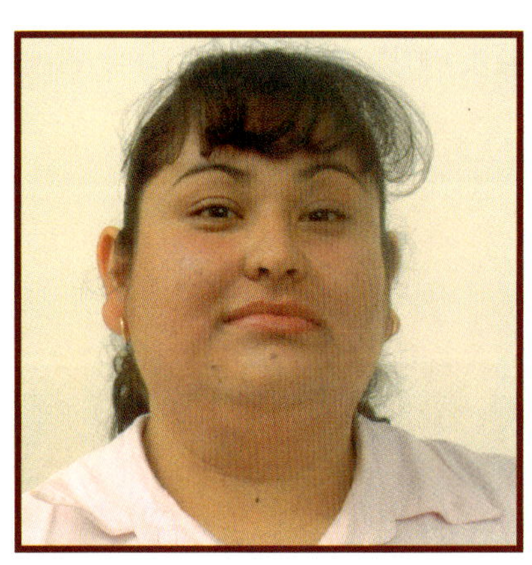

"If I can do it, you can do it too."

My Important Numbers

Doctor: ____

Phone number: ____

Pharmacist:____

Phone number: ____

Nurse:____

Phone number: ____

Diabetes Educator: ____________________________________

Phone number: ____

Family member: _______________________________________

Phone number: ____

Other:____

Acknowledgements

The development of the *Living with Diabetes: An Everyday Guide for You and Your Family* was funded by an unrestricted educational grant from Novo Nordisk.

Living with Diabetes: An Everyday Guide for You and Your Family was developed with the help of people with diabetes, their family members and health care providers under the direction of the following health care providers:

Terry Davis, PhD[1], Darren DeWalt, MD, MPH[2], Hilary Seligman, MD, MAS[3], Dean Schillinger, MD[3], Connie Arnold, PhD[1], Betsy Bryant Shilliday, PharmD, CDE, CPP[2], Nikki Bengal, BA[3], Andrea Wallace, RN, ND, PhD[2], Adriana Delgadillo, BS[3], Jorge Palacios, MSP[3] and Kathryn Davis, BA[1]

1. Louisiana State University Health Sciences Center, Shreveport
2. University of North Carolina at Chapel Hill
3. University of California, San Francisco General Hospital

Since its incorporation in 1999, the American College of Physicians Foundation's primary goal has been to provide patients with the information they need to manage and understand their health. *Living with Diabetes: An Everyday Guide for You and Your Family* was a 2-year project to develop a guide to promote patient self-management in diabetes.

AMERICAN COLLEGE OF PHYSICIANS
FOUNDATION

Graphic Design by Lewis Kalmbach
Kalmbach Advertising, Inc.
02/07-120